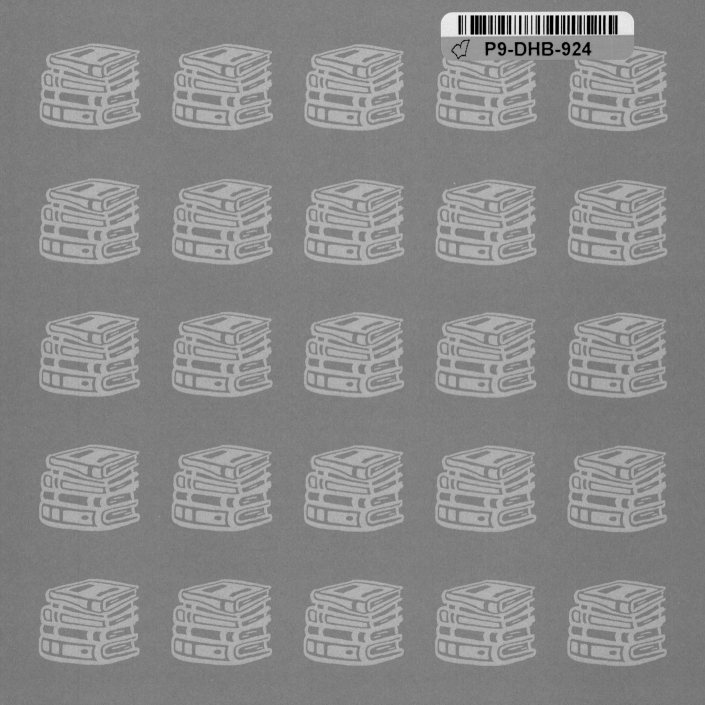

ORDINARY
PEOPLE
CHANGE
the
WORLD

I am
Martin Luther King, Jr.

BRAD MELTZER
illustrated by **Christopher Eliopoulos**

 DIAL BOOKS FOR YOUNG READERS

I am **Martin Luther King, Jr.**

When I was little, I used to get into a lot of accidents.
One day, my little brother hit me in the head with a baseball bat.
Two other times, I mistakenly got knocked over by a car.
Another day, I tumbled over our banister, then bounced through
an open door into the basement.

No matter how many
times I fell, I kept getting
back up.

Even before I could read, I knew I liked books.
My dad always talked about how I kept a lot of books around me.
I used to tell my parents:

WHEN I GROW UP I'M GOING TO GET ME SOME BIG WORDS.

There is a power in words.
Big words were in my future.

When I was six years old, one of my best friends was a boy whose father owned a store across the street.

My friend was white; I was black. It didn't matter to us. We would play games and have fun together.

But when we started going to school, everything changed.
He went to a school where all the kids were white.
I went to a school where everyone was black.
Soon after, he told me . . .

I didn't understand.
It didn't make sense.

At dinner, my parents explained . . .

IT'S BECAUSE YOU'RE BLACK AND HE'S WHITE.

I was so mad that day.

HOW COULD SOMEONE TREAT ME DIFFERENTLY JUST BECAUSE OF THE COLOR OF MY SKIN?

I wanted to hate my friend and his father.

But my parents told me to do the opposite: that I should love my friend, even though he hurt me. They taught me that it's better to have more love in your life than more hate.

Then my mother taught me one of the most important lessons of all.

YOU ARE AS GOOD AS ANYONE.

YOU MUST NEVER FEEL THAT YOU ARE LESS THAN ANYONE ELSE.

I wanted to believe it, but every day, I saw the opposite. I saw you could be treated unfairly just because of the color of your skin.

If you were white, you went to a good school, with great playgrounds and plenty of books.

If you were black, your school was small, sometimes with no desks or even windows.

It wasn't just the schools. Black people had to use different water fountains, different elevators, even different bathrooms.

In fact, on a hot day when everyone wanted ice cream, if you were white, you could sit at the counter and eat from a nice dish.

But since I was black, if they served me at all, it was through a side window, and they put my ice cream in a flimsy paper cup.

It got even worse when I was fourteen.

I had just won a speech competition. My speech was about being fair to all people.

I was so excited.

Then, on the bus ride home, a few white people got on board.

At first, I stayed put. It didn't seem fair.

But my teacher convinced me to move.

We spent the rest of the ride standing and getting tossed in every direction.

Every day, this is what life was like. Black people were treated terribly. The only question was . . .

What could I do about it?
At the age of fifteen, I started college.
By nineteen, I became a minister and entered
seminary school to study religion.

It was a lesson I wanted to share
with everyone.

In no time at all, I got my chance.

In Alabama, a black woman named Rosa Parks was told to give up her bus seat to a white man. It was just like what happened to me.

But unlike me, Mrs. Parks refused. She was arrested.

Early the next morning, I got a phone call from a local community leader.

It was just like Thoreau taught.

Instead of using violence to protest the unfair rules, black people would use a peaceful method: We would not ride the public buses.

Without our money, the bus companies would go out of business.

Now the only question was: Would it work?

On the first day of the protest, my wife called me to the window.

We had to keep it going. As the head of the bus boycott, I gave one of the most important speeches of my life.

The room was packed. Camera crews were filming.
I had only twenty minutes to prepare. I didn't use notes.
But by speaking from my heart, I found out how "big"
words can be.

The police put me in jail, saying I was breaking the law.
Other folks bombed my house.
But instead of using my fists, I kept my calm.

For more than a full year, every black person in the city, and some white people too, refused to ride the buses.
That meant some people had to walk for miles, but they kept going.
There was a power in standing together.
Eventually, our peaceful protest worked. The rules were changed.
Public buses could no longer separate people based on the color of their skin.

That was only the beginning.

Soon, our peaceful protests sparked other peaceful protests.

At lunch counters, college students organized "sit-ins," where they would not stop until everyone could eat together.

Our methods of nonviolence were so powerful, I was invited to meet with the president at the White House.

But sometimes, the hardest problems were right at home.

Seeing my daughter cry was one of the most painful moments of my life.

It only made me work harder for change.

Was it easy? Absolutely not.
During one protest in Birmingham, Alabama, the police again arrested me and locked me in a dark jail cell that had only one window.

Someone slipped me a newspaper, in which white religious leaders had written an article calling us "law breakers."
Someone then snuck me a pen.
In that jail cell, I wrote my own response in the margins of the newspaper and even on toilet paper.

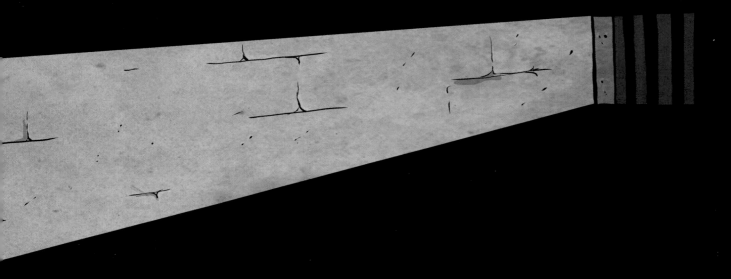

My Letter from Birmingham Jail was soon published as a pamphlet.
Then it was in magazines and newspapers.
Today, it has been read by millions of people.
Like I said, it is amazing how *big* words can be.

Our message was so important, even kids your age joined us. In Birmingham, during the Children's Crusade, more than 1,000 kids—some as young as six years old—showed up to march.

The first day, the police arrested 900 of them.
The next day, 2,500 children showed up, ready to go to jail.

This was our finest hour.

Enraged that we were not giving up, the chief of police told the firemen to spray the children with water hoses and attack them with dogs.

They thought it would stop us.

But instead, as the whole country watched on TV what they were doing to our children, it was a wake-up call for the nation's conscience.

Ninety days later, the rules began to change.

Now blacks and whites in Birmingham were using the same lunch counters, water fountains, and restrooms.

You could feel it in the air . . .

More change was coming.

Freedom was contagious.

By the summer of 1963, an estimated one million Americans held their own protests in cities across the country.

A man named A. Philip Randolph suggested a massive march.

People came from almost every state.
They came in nearly every form of transportation.
They even took off work, and did not get paid, just to be there.
Old people, young people, black people, white people—even children like you—they all came to Washington, DC, gathering in a righteous army.

Why?
Because they wanted a change.
And they knew, the surest way to change the world is to stand together.

I AM HAPPY TO JOIN WITH YOU TODAY IN WHAT WILL GO DOWN IN HISTORY AS THE GREATEST DEMONSTRATION FOR FREEDOM IN THE HISTORY OF OUR NATION.

On August 28, 1963, I stood at the podium—and spoke what some later called my "biggest" words of all.

MARCH ON WASHINGTON FOR JOBS & FREEDOM

After the March on Washington, the president and Congress passed new laws for civil rights, but that didn't mean our work was done.

Indeed, our greatest battle was still to come.

It began with 600 activists as they tried to walk fifty-four miles from Selma, Alabama, to the state capital of Montgomery.

Back then, there were rules that stopped black people from voting. If you want to *change* the laws, you have to be able to vote for new people who *make* the laws.

The police had billy clubs and tear gas.

They attacked our group and knocked many people down.

But—as I learned so long ago—you have to get back up.

No matter how hard they hit us, we remained peaceful.

Still, we didn't get through.

Two days later, we tried again.
Now there were 2,500 of us.

Once again, we tried.
Once again, we did not get through.
Did we give up?

What do *you* think?

It was Sunday, March 21, 1965: Our third try.
Now we had 8,000 people with us.

For two days, we marched.
Rain could not stop us.
The world was watching. The White House was too.
President Johnson even sent troops to protect us.

Exhaustion could not stop us.
As we reached Montgomery, Alabama, tears were shed.
But this time, they were tears of joy.

In my life, people tried to tell me I wasn't as good as they were, just because of the color of my skin.

When someone hurts you like that, it can be tempting to hurt them back.

You must refuse.

When someone shows you hate, show them love.

When someone shows you violence, show them kindness.

To reach our goals, we must walk
the path of peace.
    We must lock arms with our brothers
and sisters.
    We must march together.
    When we do . . .

I am Martin Luther King, Jr.

I stand for peace.

I stand for justice.

I stand to help others.

I stand as proof that no matter how hard the struggle, we must fight for what is right and work to change what is wrong.

Whatever struggle you face, no matter how hard it gets,
you must always move forward.
I am proof of this.
If we rise up,
if we stand together,
if we remain united,
nothing can stop our dream.

"The time is always right to do right."
—**Martin Luther King, Jr.**

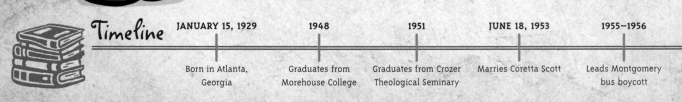

Timeline

| **JANUARY 15, 1929** | **1948** | **1951** | **JUNE 18, 1953** | **1955–1956** |
| Born in Atlanta, Georgia | Graduates from Morehouse College | Graduates from Crozer Theological Seminary | Marries Coretta Scott | Leads Montgomery bus boycott |

At the March
on Washington

Martin with his wife
and children

APRIL 16, 1963	AUGUST 28, 1963	DECEMBER 10, 1964	MARCH 21–25, 1965	APRIL 4, 1968	1986
Writes Letter from Birmingham Jail	"I Have a Dream" speech at the March on Washington	Receives Nobel Peace Prize	Selma to Montgomery March	Killed in Memphis, Tennessee	Martin Luther King, Jr. Day first observed

For my father-in-law,
Bobby Flam,
who at Jumbo's Restaurant
had the strength to fight for Dr. King's message.
I love you for what you've done for me;
I admire you for what you've done for others.
—B.M.

For my brother-in-law, James Verde.
Jippy, I consider you a brother and one of the
most caring, thoughtful people on this planet.
You always put those you love before yourself.
You're my hero.
—C.E.

For historical accuracy, we used Dr. King's actual dialogue whenever possible. For more of Dr. King's true voice, we recommend and acknowledge *The Autobiography of Martin Luther King, Jr.*, edited by Clayborne Carson.

Special thanks to Representative John Lewis, Bacardi Jackson, Michele Norris, and Brad Desnoyer for reading early drafts.

. . . .

SOURCES

The Autobiography of Martin Luther King, Jr., edited by Clayborne Carson (Warner, 2001)
Let the Trumpet Sound: A Life of Martin Luther King, Jr., by Stephen B. Oates (Harper Perennial, 2013)
Stride Toward Freedom: The Montgomery Story by Martin Luther King, Jr. (Beacon Press, 2010)
Where Do We Go From Here?: Chaos or Community? by Martin Luther King, Jr. (Beacon Press, 2010)
March: Book One by John Lewis, Andrew Aydin, and Nate Powell (Top Shelf Productions, 2013)

FURTHER READING FOR KIDS

Who Was Martin Luther King, Jr.? by Bonnie Bader (Grosset & Dunlap, 2008)
Martin's Big Words: The Life of Dr. Martin Luther King, Jr., by Doreen Rappaport (Hyperion, 2001)
I Have a Dream by Martin Luther King, Jr. (Schwartz & Wade, 2012)
My Dream of Martin Luther King by Faith Ringgold (Dragonfly, 1998)

. . . .

DIAL BOOKS FOR YOUNG READERS
Penguin Young Readers Group • An imprint of Penguin Random House, LLC
375 Hudson Street, New York, NY 10014

Text copyright © 2016 by Forty-four Steps, Inc. • Illustrations copyright © 2016 by Christopher Eliopoulos

Library of Congress Cataloging-in-Publication Data
Meltzer, Brad.
I am Martin Luther King, Jr. / Brad Meltzer ; illustrated by Christopher Eliopoulos
pages cm. — (Ordinary people change the world) • Summary: "A biography of Martin Luther King, Jr. that tells the story of how he used nonviolence to lead the civil rights movement"— Provided by publisher. • ISBN 978-0-525-42852-7 (hardback) • 1. King, Martin Luther, Jr., 1929–1968—Juvenile literature. 2. African Americans—Biography—Juvenile literature. 3. Civil rights workers—United States—Biography—Juvenile literature. 4. African Americans—Civil rights—History—20th century—Juvenile literature. 5. Civil rights movements—United States—History—20th century—Juvenile literature. 6. Nonviolence—United States—History—20th century—Juvenile literature. I. Eliopoulos, Chris, illustrator. II. Title. • E185.97.K5M398 2016   323.092—dc23   [B]   2015015141

Photo on page 38 © Flip Schulke/Corbis. Page 39: March on Washington photo © Hulton-Deutsch Collection/Corbis; Family photo © Globe Photos/ZUMA Press/Corbis

Printed in China • 10 9 8 7 6 5 4 3 2 1
Designed by Jason Henry • Text set in Triplex • The artwork for this book was created digitally.

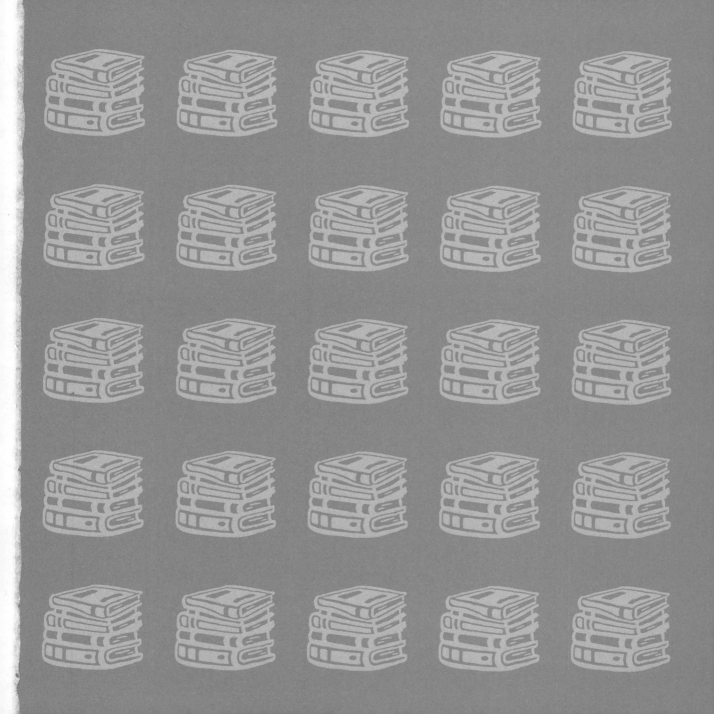

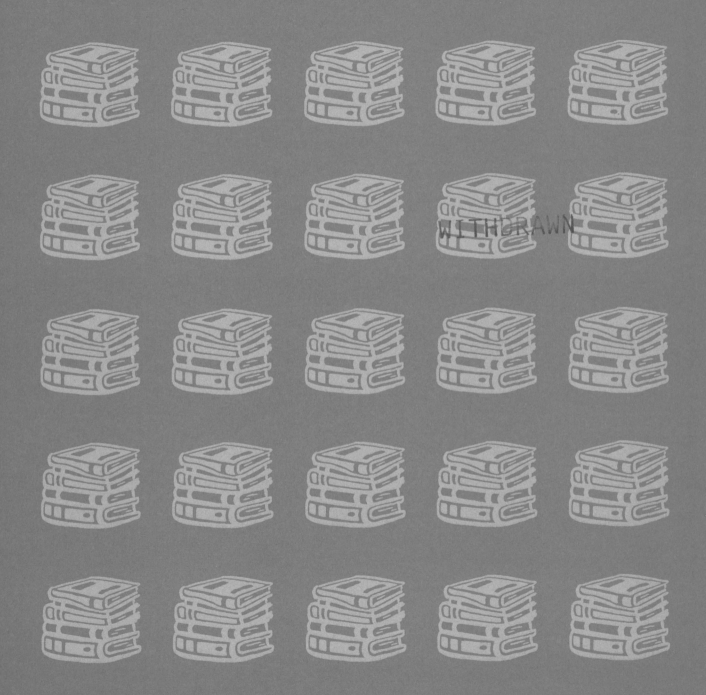